Cats Are Better Than Dogs

ALSO BY MISSY DIZICK :

CAT SCAN

RUSSLE

DOGS ARE BETTER THAN CATS

Cats Are Better Than Dogs

Missy Dizick

DOUBLEDAY

NEW YORK LONDON TORONTO SYDNEY AUCKLAND

PUBLISHED BY DOUBLEDAY
A DIVISION OF BANTAM DOUBLEDAY DELL PUBLISHING GROUP, INC.
1540 BROADWAY, NEW YORK, NEW YORK 10036

DOUBLEDAY AND THE PORTRAYAL OF AN ANCHOR WITH A DOLPHIN ARE TRADEMARKS
OF DOUBLEDAY, A DIVISION OF BANTAM DOUBLEDAY DELL PUBLISHING GROUP, INC.

LIBRARY OF CONGRESS CATALOGING-IN-PUBLICATION DATA

CATS ARE BETTER THAN DOGS! / MISSY DIZICK. — 1ST ED.
P. CM.
1. CATS—CARICATURES AND CARTOONS. 2. AMERICAN WIT AND HUMOR,
PICTORIAL.   I. TITLE
NC1429.D548A4   1993
741.5'973—DC20   92-38298
                                      CIP

ISBN 0-385-46848-2

TO ALL THE PRECIOUS LITTLE PUSSYCATS

IN THE WHOLE WIDE WORLD, ESPECIALLY

LOULOU AND THE LATE MABLE WHISKERS

Cats Are Better Than Dogs

CAT: WARM SOFT FURRY THING WITH MOTOR RUNNING. CAN B

PLACED ON PERSON AS DESIRED. ADD MORE AS NEEDED.

DOG: OBSEQUIOUS SYCOPHANT, LACKING IN CRITICAL JUDGMENT.

CATS ARE SELF-TRAINING.

DOGS ARE ACCIDENT-PRONE.

CATS APPRECIATE THAT LIFE BRINGS THINGS IN TIME.

DOGS FETCH.

CATS ALWAYS LAND ON THEIR FEET.

DOGS DON'T.

CATS ARE SELF-CLEANING.

DOGS ARE HIGH-MAINTENANCE.

CATS PLAY TRICKS.

DOGS DO TRICKS.

CATS GET HAIRBALLS.

DOGS SWALLOW LARGE FOREIGN BODIES, AND GO T

SURGERY.

CATS HUNT.

DOGS ASSIST.

CATS STARING INTO SPACE ARE: 1) CONTEMPLATING THE

NIVERSE; 2)COMMUNING WITH SPIRITS; 3)PLANNING A KILL.

DOGS STARING INTO SPACE ARE: STARING INTO SPACE.

CATS ARE MODELS OF STRESS MANAGEMENT AND RELAXATION

TECHNIQUE.

DOGS ARE EITHER WORKAHOLICS OR VANDALS.

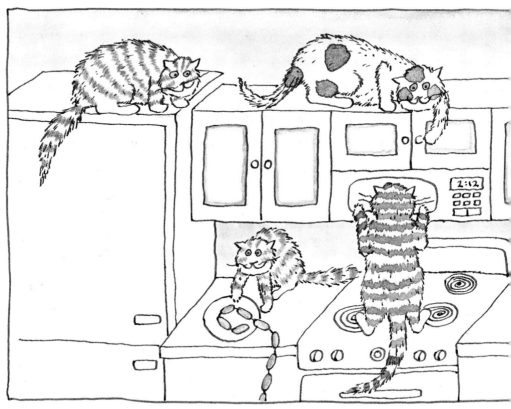

CATS CAN GO GET THINGS FOR THEMSELVES.

DOGS NEED HELP,

CATS MAKE FRIENDS WITH VISITORS.

DOGS COMMIT MAYHEM ON METER READERS, DELIVERY

PERSONS, AND OTHER DOGS.

A GALLERY OF BEAUTIFULLY DESIGNED CATS.

A GALLERY OF BADLY DESIGNED DOGS.

WHAT WE'LL NEVER DO IS HEEL
CHASING CARS HAS GREAT APPEAL
GROWL AT BABIES, MAKE 'EM SQUEAL
ROTTEN THINGS, OUR FAVORITE MEAL

ABOUT THE AUTHOR

MISSY DIZICK, WHO LIVES IN NAPA, CALIFORNIA, IS THE ILLUSTRATOR OF <u>CAT SCAN</u>, AND THE AUTHOR/ILLUSTRATOR OF <u>RUSSLE</u> AND <u>DOGS ARE BETTER THAN CATS</u> (WITH MARY BLY). HER PRIZE-WINNING ARTWORK APPEARS ON POSTERS, NOTE CARDS, AND CALENDARS, AND HAS BEEN SHOWN IN GALLERIES AND MUSEUMS IN CALIFORNIA AND NEW YORK.